806

A PERSONAL PERSPECTIVE ON IRISH PEN

A *Personal Perspective on* Irish PEN

J. Anthony Gaughan

KINGDOM

BOOKS

Designed and typeset in 12/16 on 14 point Scala by SUSAN WAINE
Printed in Ireland

Published by
KINGDOM BOOKS
56 NEWTOWNPARK AVENUE • BLACKROCK
COUNTY DUBLIN • IRELAND

First published in 2019

ISBN: 978-1-9164764-1-7

Front cover:
TOP ROW: Brian Friel, Seámus Heaney, Maurice Walsh.
MIDDLE ROW: Edna O'Brien, Maeve Binchy, Ann Enright.
BOTTOM ROW: Brendan Kennelly, Bryan MacMahon, John B. Keane.

ACKNOWLEDGEMENTS

I was prompted to compile this account of Irish PEN following a request to provide an essay on the Centre for the forthcoming International PEN centenary celebration in 2021.

In connection with the preparation of the booklet, I wish to thank Ginevra Avalle, Secretary of the Centenary Archive Collection, for much useful information.

For additions, corrections and suggestions my thanks are due to Stephen Collins, Mgr Martin Cummins, Marita Conlon-McKenna, Liam Murphy, Fr Michael O'Connor and Vanessa Fox-O'Loughlin.

A special word of thanks to Loretto Dalton who encouraged me to write the booklet and assisted in preparing it for publication.

I am most grateful to Pádraig Hanratty and Felix Larkin for their rigorous editing of my original draft.

I wish to thank Jennifer Clement, President, PEN International for writing an excellent Afterword.

Most of all, I wish to thank President Michael D. Higgins for his splendid message to Irish PEN and the world-wide PEN community.

Finally, I am indebted to Susan Waine for the layout and design of the booklet and to Ray Lynn for printing it.

To

The Imprisoned Writer

*"I detest what you write, but I would give my life
to make it possible for you to continue to write"*

VOLTAIRE

Contents

SOURCES

Dublin, National Library of Ireland
Ms 49,141 (Irish PEN papers, 1935 – 2004)
In private hands
Papers of J. Anthony Gaughan

Foreword

THE HISTORY OF PEN International is a long and illustrious one. Founded almost a century ago with the aim of promoting friendship and intellectual co-operation amongst writers of all nationalities, today PEN is active in over 100 countries across the globe. The organisation has not only made a profound contribution to the strengthening of connections between our large international community of writers, but has also worked tirelessly to fight the censorship and oppression faced by writers and journalists in countries where those who exercise the fundamental human right of speaking out and expressing their view face harassment, intimidation, imprisonment and death.

The Irish branch of PEN, informally set up by Lady Gregory in 1921 and formalised thirteen years later in 1931 has, across the intervening decades, received the membership and support of an impressive roll call of Ireland's most renowned and best loved writers. Seán O'Faoláin described the purpose of its Irish foundation as being:

> "to feel the rivalry, the emulation, the excitement of ideas, of criticism, of everything that belongs to the world of imagination and ideas ... we recognize and fight for the intellectual fraternity of mankind."

Those stirring and inspiring words continue to describe the spirit that lies at the heart of Irish PEN, an organisation that unites its' voice with its fellow PEN centres around the world in expressing solidarity with all those who use the written word to challenge the status quo, and to question the world around us.

We in Ireland are very fortunate that we can speak and write freely without fear or oppression. But we must never forget the many brave writers who are unjustly persecuted and terrorised for their peacefully expressed views. By standing in unity with them, Irish PEN is also standing in unison with all those who are denied their entitlement, under the Human Declaration of Human Rights, to:

> "hold opinions without interference and to seek, receive and impart information and ideas through any media and regardless of frontiers".

As a nation we can be deeply grateful to Irish PEN for upholding the written word as a crucial vehicle for citizen participation and viable democracy, and for taking a stand against the denial of freedom of expression to fellow writers around the world, a denial which is an attack on the very notion of truth itself.

MICHAEL D. HIGGINS
Uachtarán na hÉireann

CHAPTER ONE

Member of Irish PEN

I JOINED IRISH PEN in January 1974. This I did at the request of John B. Keane, who served as its president from 1973 to 1977. Irish PEN is a branch of International P.E.N., a worldwide association of writers. PEN brings together poets, novelists, essayists, historians, playwrights, critics, translators, editors, journalists and screenwriters in a common concern for the craft of writing, to give expression to their commitment to freedom of expression and to promote international good will among writers generally. Through its 149 centres in more than 100 countries, it operates on all continents.

It was founded in London in 1921 by the novelist Catherine Amy Dawson Scott. She sent the following notice to potential members: 'London has no centre where well-known writers of both sexes can meet, no place where visitors from abroad can hope to find them. A dinner club would enable them to meet socially without being under obligation to anyone. The qualifications for membership are: (a) A book of verse published by a well-known continental, London or American firm; (b) A play produced by any well-known theatre; (c) The editorship,

past or present, of a well-known newspaper or magazine;
(d) A novel published by a well-known London,
continental or American firm. Membership subscription
5/- [five shillings] yearly'.

Forty-one writers attended the inaugural dinner at a
restaurant in Piccadilly on 5 October 1921 and joined the
new PEN club. Thereafter they were known as the
'Foundation Members' and included Joseph Conrad, John
Galsworthy and D.H. Lawrence. Later, prominent writers
in continental Europe and North America were
approached with a view to establishing centres in their
own countries. The response from most of them,
including Maxim Gorky in Russia, Anatole France in
France and Edith Wharton in the US, was positive and
soon the organisation became international with its
administrative centre in London.

Marjorie Watts, PEN's first secretary and daughter of
its founder, wrote to Lady Augusta Gregory in Dublin
suggesting that she summon writers together to form a
centre in Ireland. This attempt to establish a PEN centre
in Ireland with Lady Gregory as president was not entirely
successful. It seems that the Irish writers were in the main
solitary characters, not given to joining organisations or
discussing their work. This attitude was not uncommon
among the best-known writers. When George Bernard
Shaw was invited to preside at an English PEN dinner his
reply was typically Shavian: 'Galsworthy was pulling your
leg. He knows that I abhor literary society. As to presiding
at a literary dinner words fail me! You can't really have
enjoyed that foolish crowd at Stratford'. But Shaw joined

PEN in 1924 yielding to John Galsworthy's persuasion as follows: 'Whitemailer! Very well, I will go quietly. It's your doing, though, but I will not face a recurrent irritation of a guinea a year. Here is twenty guineas for a life subscription (I am 68). If they won't accept that they can make me an honorary member, and be damned to them'.

The second attempt to establish a PEN centre in Ireland was more successful. This was spearheaded by Bulmer Hobson, Lord Longford and Seán Ó Faoláin in 1934. Parallel centres were set up in Belfast and Dublin thus providing a link between Irish writers north and south. By 1940 Irish PEN had over 130 members, more than a hundred belonging to the Dublin centre.

Most of the best-known Irish writers since then have been members of PEN. These include John Banville, Maeve Binchy, Clare Boylan, Brian Cleeve, Fr Desmond Forristal, Monk Gibbon, Jennifer Johnston, Mary Lavin, J.J. Lee, Walter Macken, Edward MacLysaght, Bryan MacMahon, Brinsley MacNamara, Conor Cruise O'Brien, Edna O'Brien, Kate O'Brien, Frank O'Connor, Peader O'Donnell, Liam O'Flaherty, Francis Stuart, Alice Taylor, and Maurice Walsh. Playwrights have been represented by Maurice Davin Power, Bernard Farrell, Brian Friel, Denis Johnston, John B. Keane, Hugh Leonard and Frank McGuinness. And the names of poets such as Eavan Boland, Austin Clarke, John F. Deane and Séamus Heaney are also on the rolls of Irish PEN

Not having a premises of its own Irish PEN has had to conduct meetings at various venues. Initially meetings were held in Robert Roberts literary cafe in Grafton Street.

Later they were held in the office of *Dublin Opinion* and in a meeting room of the Royal Dublin Society. For the most part, appropriately enough, they have been and are still generally held in the United Arts Club. In the 1940s and 1950s meetings were occasionally convened in the homes of members of the executive committee, following a sherry reception.

One of the most memorable dates in the early history of Irish PEN was 27 June 1935, when the centre organised a dinner on the seventieth birthday of W.B.Yeats. The venue was the Hibernian Hotel, where the ballroom was transformed into a banqueting hall. One contempory press report described Yeats with his white mane sitting serenely at the top table listening to an address by John Masefield, the poet laureate of the United Kingdom. The toast was to 'Ireland and Yeats' and glowing tributes were paid to Yeats by his contemporaries.

Ireland was the location for the 25th and 38th International PEN Congresses in 1953 and 1971. The latter assembly met on the golden jubilee of the association and its theme was 'The changing face of literature: a discussion and evaluation of developments over the past fifty years'. Five hundred delegates attended the congress in the Royal Marine Hotel, Dún Laoghaire. At the opening ceremony, the then Taoiseach, Jack Lynch, TD, described the gathering as 'a world assembly of men and women of letters'. He recalled that, when PEN was founded, Dublin was the centre of a remarkable literary revival; 'Synge was only a few years dead, Yeats was at the height of his power and Joyce was putting the finishing touches to *Ulysses*'. In

his closing address the international president, Heinrich
Böll, paid an exceptionally warm tribute to Irish PEN for
their successful organisation of the congress.

Subsequently the committee arranged for the
publication of *The changing face of literature: a discussion of
developments over the first fifty years* – a collection of the
lectures given at the congress. Desmond Clarke in his
annual report for 1973 – 74 noted that it had sold very well
and had augmented considerably the funds held by the
Centre.

Irish PEN has fought for many causes. Censorship in
general and the censorship of books in particular were
ever-recurring themes for discussion at meetings. The
Centre took a strong line against a strange ban on the
importation of Irish books into England. It successfully
sought for legislation to ensure that writers would be paid
for the use of their books in libraries. The Centre
communicated with the Russian Embassy concerning an
unsatisfactory position in regard to royalties due to Irish
writers whose works had been translated into Russian.
Irish PEN petitioned the Taoiseach to introduce a pension
scheme for artists, writers and poets who had fallen on
bad times, similar to the Aosdána arrangement which was
eventually inaugurated. Occasionally it became involved
in issues concerning copyright. It successfully
campaigned to have writers adequately represented on the
Arts Council.

The longest campaign conducted by the Centre
concerned taxation on books. Value Added Tax (VAT) was
introduced in Ireland in 1972 as a consequence of

Ireland's impending entry to the European Economic Community (EEC). Books were initially charged at a rate of 5.26%, the rate increased to 10% in 1976 and to 15% in 1981. Eventually after the persistent canvassing by Irish PEN and others the government removed the VAT on books in 1982. And year after year the Centre was in communication with hotels, airports and display centres requesting that books by Irish writers be prominently displayed in all their book racks.

I was elected to the executive committee of Irish PEN in May 1976. Charles E. Kelly was both chairman and president at the time. He had held many senior posts in the civil service, including that of director of broadcasting. But he will always be associated with *Dublin Opinion*.

This satirical monthly was founded by Arthur Booth in 1922. Following his death Charlie Kelly with Tom Collins co-edited it from 1926 to 1968. Many of the cartoons in *Dublin Opinion* were brilliant but CEK, as Charlie signed his work, had his own niche in social commentary. Even up to the 1970s people recalled their favourite CEK cartoons. There was the depiction of the night that the Kildare Street Club held a *céilí*. Charlie had lots of fun with the diminutive Séan T. O'Kelly. The latter in a speech after the 1938 Anglo-Irish Agreement which ended the so-called 'Economic War' claimed publicly that we had 'whipped John Bull'. For a long time afterwards, Charlie depicted him with a whip hanging out of his back pocket. He presented an elongated de Valera 'The Long Fellow' with a sly and mischievous gleam in his eye. His cartoon on the cover of *Dublin Opinion* for August 1942, which reflected the widespread influence of Alfred O'Rahilly's sustained and occasional intemperate attacks on the Central Bank Bill, had the hallmark of genius.

Charlie's humour and that of the *Dublin Opinion* was a satire in words and drawings which had bite but little or no rancour. It laughed at the Irish Free State's new institutions and political bodies and its politicians, but everyone – including the victims of its humour - laughed along with them. Although in the early years of the new State there was much to be grateful for and much hope for a better future, there was also confusion and a great deal of strife and hatred, arising from the civil war. In that context the appearance of the saucy *Dublin Opinion* and Charlie's cartoons were more than timely for it was important to help Ireland laugh and laugh in a wholesome way.

It has frequently been stated that many of those who write and perform comedy are sad and lonely people. At PEN meetings Charlie was always in high good humour and obviously a person who enjoyed company. But I was surprised at how seldom he indulged in humorous exchanges or repartee.

Desmond Clarke and Barbara Walsh, as members of the committee, did more than most in terms of organisation. Desmond was the librarian at the Royal Dublin Society and acted as secretary to Irish PEN for many years. Barbara was the treasurer. They later exchanged roles. As secretary, Barbara established links with the Society of Irish Playwrights and Clé, the Irish Book Publishers Association, and had members of these bodies serve on the committee. It was generally recognised that Desmond and Barbara were responsible for the remarkable success of the Irish Centre's golden jubilee congress and celebrations.

Dorine Rohan had her career as a writer and her membership of the committee cut short by a horrific accident which left her seriously disabled. Constantine FitzGibbon, an expatriate American, attended meetings only occasionally and, it seemed to me, generally after a protracted lunch. Alan Llewellyn was an eccentric Welshman. A very large man, he had an extraordinarily high-pitched voice and tended to be over-sensitive.

Rita O'Brien had spent a lifetime promoting the arts. She was as interested in the visual arts as she was in literature and had established an art gallery near the former Hell-Fire Club in the Dublin mountains which had a cult status for a number of years.

Irene Haugh, Mary Lavin and Eithne Strong also served on the committee. Of these Mary Lavin was the best known, mainly for her short stories. There was the poet, John F. Deane. Tall, with thin features, he had a long beard and the appearance of an ascetic. By contrast John Ryan's appearance left us in no doubt that he was a *bon vivant*. Better known as a broadcaster than as a writer, he was at the time attempting to launch a literary magazine.

For me the most interesting member of the committee was Bryan Walter Guinness, Lord Moyne. He was the oldest son of Walter Edward Guinness, first Baron Moyne. In 1944 he had succeeded his father as second Baron Moyne and was known as Lord Moyne. He had had a few books of poetry published and was respected as a poet. At meetings he was rather quaintly referred to as Moyne.

Although he was well able to hold his ground in argument, he was a gentle and very likeable person. In the late 1970s and early 1980s the conflict in Northern Ireland was becoming more and more tragic. On a number of occasions, I proposed that Irish PEN should take a public stand in the matter and, in effect, urge the British authorities to aim for a political rather than a military solution to the civil unrest and at times open warfare. In the event, most of the committee members were opposed to any public intervention on the grounds that it would mean straying into the area of politics which was not countenanced in the constitution of PEN. So Irish PEN maintained a silence on the subject.

When this matter was discussed Lord Moyne cogently and vigorously argued a counter-view to mine. After two such sessions he invited me to continue the discussion over lunch at his imposing residence, 'Knockmaroon House', near Chapelizod. These occasions were more convivial than when Lord Moyne, in conjunction with Irish PEN, hosted at his home a special tribute evening for the distinguished and inebriated writer, Liam O'Flaherty, on the latter's 85th birthday.

Apart from Irish PEN, Lord Moyne was involved in other cultural activities. He was a prominent member of the Irish Association for Cultural, Economic and Social Relations. Under its aegis a group drawn from Britain, Northern Ireland and the Republic of Ireland met to promote co-operation and good-will between the three jurisdictions. Their meetings were held in London, Belfast and in the Friendly Brothers Club, St Stephen's Green, Dublin.

When Lord Moyne read my biography of Tom Johnson he invited me to give a talk to this group on the Labour leader. Apart from being flattered by the invitation, I was immensely gratified that the event was a cause of considerable pleasure to Mrs Kathleen Johnson, Tom Johnson's daughter-in-law. Kathleen was the manager of the bar in the Friendly Brothers Club. Throughout her life she had been closer to Johnson than even his wife, Marie, and she was delighted that the achievements and stature of 'Pops', as she referred to him, were being discussed in such influential company.

Lord Moyne continued to be a member of the executive committee of Irish PEN until mid-1985, when, owing to ill-health, he resigned. However, I am fortunate to have a signed copy of his poems which he had presented to me to remember him by.

CHAPTER TWO

Chairman of Irish PEN

IN APRIL 1981 I was elected chairman of the executive committee of Irish PEN. which by that time represented only the Dublin Centre. Owing to the serious civil unrest in Northern Ireland, the Belfast Centre had been dormant from 1974 onwards and eventually in 1977 it was disbanded and some of its members joined the Dublin Centre. The last significant event organised by the Belfast Centre was a two-day seminar it arranged with the Dublin Centre in 1973 at which the principal speakers were Eavan Boland, John Broderick, Hugh Leonard and Charles E. Kelly. In 1981 Arthur Flynn became the honorary secretary of Irish PEN. As interested in the theatre as in literature, Arthur was already a member of the Society of Irish Playwrights and from 1985 onwards served as treasurer of that Society which in 2001 became the Irish Playwrights & Screenwriters Guild. Apart from his writing and deep interest in film-making in Ireland, Arthur mainly concerned himself with drafting plays for radio. Arthur set about recruiting new members. He also enthusiastically pursued members who had not paid their annual subscriptions. The greatest offenders in this regard were generally members with the highest profiles!

During his second year in office Arthur was active in enhancing the international profile of Irish PEN. He arranged for Eithne Strong, John F. Deane and Jack Harte to be guests at a conference of the Danish Authors Association in September and he represented the Centre at the International PEN Congress in London in November. And in the meantime he and John F. Deane had contributed articles to a James Joyce centenary edition of the Dutch literary magazine *Kruispunt*.

In his annual report for 1998 – 99 Arthur addressed the topic of the Irish Centre's basic financial position. The annual subscription paid by members at that time was £18, by associates it was £15 and by unwaged £5. Then the Centre annually remitted to International PEN $15 for registered members, whether or not that person had paid his or her subscription. In appealing for subscriptions Arthur and others reminded members that International PEN was a bonding of more than one hundred Centres and over twelve thousand writers worldwide and depended for its continuance and operations on the remittance of the various Centres. And he, like everyone else in PEN, stressed its importance as an organisation dedicated not only to the freedom of writers to express their opinions but for the free and unhampered transmission of thoughts and ideas throughout the world. Arthur's commitment to PEN was edifying and for more than two decades, by virtue of his diligence and organisational skill he was largely responsible for the successful running of Irish PEN.

The principal activity of the Centre was the monthly

meeting open to members, associate members and the public. This follows a meeting of the committee and generally features a presentation from a member of the committee, an author who has just had a book published or a playwright whose play has recently been produced. Over the years there have been some memorable lectures: Barry Cassin on his reminiscences of the Irish theatre, Pat Donlon on the National Library of Ireland, Chris Fitzsimons on Hilton Edwards and Mícheál Mac Liammóir, Marian Keaney on Padraic Colum, Gus Martin and Lorna Reynolds on Yeats and David Norris on Joyce. Talent as a writer is no guarantee that a person will be an interesting public speaker. Lectures by the immensely successful writers Ian St James and Gordon Thomas promised more than they fulfilled. On these occasions the humanity and personality of the lecturers is much to the fore. I recall Garret FitzGerald, when talking about his then recently published *All in a life,* making some extraordinary claims and comments about his very early childhood.

The average attendance at meetings was just under 20. On some occasions the committee was embarrassed by the small number who had come to a lecture by a well-known writer. Only two members of the public arrived for a lecture by Peter de Rosa. A few years earlier he had given a well-attended lecture and had returned to speak on his new publication *Rebels: the Irish rising of 1916* (1990). Aware of the committee's embarrassment, before he began he recalled that some fifteen years earlier, when involved in an extramural university course, he had been deputed to travel from the south of England to the University of Hull to deliver a lecture. Two persons attended and he learned afterwards that one of them was stone-deaf!

The Centre generally had as many associate members as members who were established writers. In May 2001 it had 87 members and 77 associates. Thus one of its aims was to encourage and help aspiring writers. Apart from authors discussing their work, sessions were held on 'How to get published?'. Representatives from the publishing houses attended and replied to queries on every aspect of their trade. Without exception publishers and writers' agents were generous with their support in this regard. And at different times Michael Gill, Michael O'Brien and the affable Seán O'Boyle of Columba Press represented publishers on the committee of Irish PEN.

'The role of the critic' was discussed with the help of literary and theatre critics. Theatre directors have explained the relationship between the playwright and a director in the presentation of a play. And to promote cultural events the Centre from time to time joined with other groups, such as the Canadian Embassy, Dublin City of Culture Committee, Dublin Millennium Cultural Committee and the Goethe Institute. One of the most successful events organised by the Centre was a joint meeting in 1973 with the Goethe Institute at which the distinguished German writer Uwe Johnson was the principal speaker, with John Hewett representing the Belfast centre, Christabel Bielenberg representing the Dublin centre, and an attendance of some 150 people.

The Centre also encouraged aspiring writers by the sponsorship of prizes under its aegis. From 1983 until his death in 1996 O.Z. Whitehead, a member of the committee, presented an annual prize of £500 to the winner of a play competition. Later this competition was funded by Carolyn Swift. For a number of years a Peace Prize, valued at £350, was sponsored by Associate Member Mrs Eileen Healy. The prize was for a short story on the theme of peace. When this sponsorship lapsed it was renewed for a number of years by Ian St James.

This was not the first short story competition sponsored by the Centre. Three hundred short stories were submitted to one organised in 1970. Helen Mary Burke, a member of the staff in the sociology department in UCD, won first prize which was presented by the chairman, Judge Kenneth Deale, at a meeting in December when the prize-winning stories were read by the authors.

The Centre is honoured to be associated with the most prestigious literary prize of all: that presented by the Nobel Peace Committee in Stockholm. The committee is invited to nominate a writer for that prize. It is now no secret that Séamus Heaney almost invariably was the Centre's choice. When Heaney was awarded the Nobel Prize for Literature in 1995 the Centre in its letter of congratulation offered him honorary life membership of Irish PEN   which he graciously accepted. Previously, in 1970 honorary life membership had been granted to Kate O'Brien, Patricia Lynch, Mary Lavin, Samuel Beckett and Liam O'Flaherty.

In 1998 the Centre initiated its own prize: the A.T.

Cross/Irish PEN annual award. This award, restricted to Irish-born writers, is presented to those who have made an outstanding contribution to Irish writing. During a discussion by the committee on the Nobel Prize for Literature it was generally agreed that it was unlikely that that prize would be coming again to Ireland in the near future. Krzysztof J. Romanowski informed the meeting that in his native Poland an annual award presented by Polish PEN was regarded as second only in prestige to the Nobel Prize. His suggestion that Irish PEN should present such an award was enthusiastically endorsed. A.T. Cross, the pen manufacturer, sponsored the prize and it was presented for the first time in 1999 to John B. Keane.

The administrative office in London of International PEN keeps national Centres informed of events which affect writers in different parts of the world. In addition, at the Annual International Congress academics and writers from across the world discuss issues relevant to all writers and writing. When the Congress is held outside Europe sometimes it has not been possible for Irish PEN to be represented, largely because of the cost involved. However, when it has been convened in Europe, Ireland has generally been represented. In 1981 John F Deane attended the Congress which was jointly held in Lyon and Paris, and in 1981 and 1988 Arthur Flynn represented the Irish Centre at meetings in London and Cambridge respectively, and in 1994 Dr Maria Romanowski on behalf of the committee attended the Congress in Prague.

The 66th World Congress was held in the University of Warsaw in June 1999. Delegates from more than 70 countries attended. With Krzysztof Joseph and Maria Romanowski, I represented Irish PEN. At the request of the committee I prepared a report on the Congress to be circulated to members (for this, see appendix 1).

At every Congress writers who have been imprisoned because of expressing their ideas and views are always an important item on the agenda. However, it is not only at Congress that this topic is given priority. In almost all correspondence from the International Centre to national Centres there is news about imprisoned writers and the efforts of members of PEN to have them released or at least to draw public attention to their plight.

In 1986 Irish PEN set up a sub-committee to improve its support for these prisoners of conscience. Aisling Ní Dhonnchadha was most active in this campaign. A former lecturer in the Irish department in Our Lady of Mercy College of Education at Carysfort, Blackrock, and already a member of Amnesty International, she corresponded with prisoners and even succeeded in sending books to some of them. One of her correspondents had received a sentence of 48 years for writing articles!

In an article published in the *Irish Times* of 8 May 1986 in the series 'Beocheist', Aisling explained the importance of the campaign. She noted that, according to the report issued in the previous autumn by the Writers in Prison Committee of International PEN, 445 writers, editors or publishers were either in jail, prison camps or detained in mental institutions. Still others had simply disappeared, as a result of the determination of governments or rulers to stifle freedom of speech and the publication of the truth.

She gave the main outlines of the story of three writers who had been imprisoned: Alaide F. de Solorzano in Guatemala, Recep Marashi in Turkey and Lothar Herbst in Poland. She added that there were hundreds of similar cases in Russia, Iran, Cuba and Vietnam. Aisling quoted Nadine Gordimer: 'All the writer can do, as a writer, is to go on writing the truth as he or she sees it'. She concluded by quoting Camus and Voltaire on the obligation of all writers to speak on behalf of writers and people who were prevented from 'speaking out'.

Down through the years the prisoners Irish PEN attempted to assist were in Cuba, South Africa, Taiwan, Turkey and Uruguay. After Aisling resigned from PEN in 1991 her active concern for prisoners of conscience was continued by Susan Schreibmann. A native of New York and lecturer in the English department in UCD, her chief focus was prisoners in Cuba.

In 1990 the Centre organised the collection and transport to Romania of much-needed books after the fall of the communist regime of Nicolae Ceaucescu. In 1991, like every other Centre throughout the world, Irish PEN protested to the Iranian government about the fatwah/death threat pronounced on Salman Rushdie. This followed protests which had been made by the Centre in the spring of 1989.

Towards the end of 1990 Gerry Adams, the leading spokesperson for Sinn Féin, applied for membership of Irish PEN (see appendix 2 for Rules of Irish PEN). Traditionally the requirement for membership has been either (a) two books published professionally, (b) two plays produced professionally or (c) a book and play from each of these categories. In due course a completed form, including a listing of two books, *Falls memories* (1982) and *The politics of Irish freedom* (1986), published by Brandon Press, and the then current membership fee of £10 were received. Some members of the committee were vigorously opposed to Adams becoming a member. I argued strongly that, as he had fulfilled the requirements for membership, he was entitled to it. In the event, a majority of the committee agreed with that point of view and Adams' membership was passed in customary fashion at the monthly meeting in January 1991.

Soon afterwards Adams' membership of Irish PEN was reported in the *Evening Press*. The committee was subjected to considerable adverse criticism on the matter. Hugh Leonard was among those who were most vociferous in their objections. He publicly stated that, as a result, he was resigning from PEN, notwithstanding the fact that his membership had lapsed years earlier. He then challenged me to publicly debate the issue with him. I was glad to oblige. On a live radio programme I explained that Adams had fulfilled the requirements for membership and so was entitled to it. I also pointed out that bans, censorship and the imprisoning of writers for their views were issues on which International PEN took an unambiguous stand. Moreover I pointed out that if Salman Rushdie, who had upset millions with his views, was to apply for membership of Irish PEN he also would be accepted. Leonard's principal counter-argument was to compare Adams to Adolf Hitler!

This did not end the adverse criticism. Considerable pressure was exerted on Arthur Flynn, the secretary of Irish PEN, and he contacted the office of the International Centre for advice on the matter. They suggested that Adams should be required to sign the PEN charter. The secretary also learned that Adams had applied to American PEN for permission to enter the US, which he was banned from visiting. The International Centre further stated that they could only support him in his request if he was giving a talk or attending a writers' conference. Although not unduly surprised, members of the committee were somewhat resentful of the manner in which PEN membership was being exploited. Nonetheless, the matter was left in abeyance and Adams' membership was allowed to stand.

The membership of Gerry Adams became a live issue again in the summer of 1993 when his publisher, Steve MacDonagh of Brandon Press, challenged RTÉ's broadcasting ban on his author and sought PEN's support in this regard. By the late autumn, as the outline of the proposals proposed by Gerry Adams and John Hume for a breakthrough in the impasse in Northern Ireland became known, those who were utterly opposed to making any concessions to Sinn Féin exerted considerable pressure to maintain the ban on Adams from broadcasting and other media outlets. Even the International Centre of PEN was lobbied in an attempt to end Adams' continuing membership of Irish PEN and in response they enquired if he had signed the charter (see appendix 3). The committee decided to invite him to sign it, but I insisted that all existing members be also asked to do so. For many years this had not been insisted on as a condition for membership. I also undertook to have a message delivered to Adams that, if he wished to remain a member of PEN, it was necessary for him to sign the charter promptly! In due course he did so.

At that stage a number of developments were making it impossible to continue the broadcasting and media ban on Sinn Féin and denial of entry to the US to Adams. His membership of PEN was one of these. In retrospect I was glad that in this small way Irish PEN assisted Adams to play his crucial role with Bertie Ahern, Tony Blair, Bill Clinton, John Hume, John Major, George Mitchell, Albert Reynolds and David Trimble in the Peace Process which led to the historic Good Friday Agreement.

CHAPTER THREE

Irish PEN's Main Social Activity

HE ANNUAL PEN DINNER for members and associate members is the highlight of the Centre's events each year. Before 1981 a dinner was held only very occasionally. Soon after he became secretary Arthur Flynn easily persuaded his colleagues on the committee of the merits of such an event, not least in order to raise the public profile of Irish PEN. Since then with just one exception the dinner has been held each year and its success has largely been due to the secretary.

At least two visitors are invited to the dinner, one as the guest of honour, the other as principal speaker. Over the years I have felt immensely privileged in acting, with the rest of the committee, as host to a wide variety of distinguished and interesting persons. In November 1981 the guest of honour was Charles J. Haughey, then leader of the Opposition. Both Arthur Flynn and I found Haughey taciturn and seemingly in a rather troubled state of mind. By contrast Sam McAughtry, the principal speaker, was delightful company. At that time McAughtry was writing a column in the *Irish Times* and had for some of the readers almost a cult status. He was also well-known for his broadcasts on RTÉ radio.

PRESIDENTS OF IRISH PEN:

Left: Maurice Walsh (1879 – 1964),
Below left: Charles E. Kelly (1902 – 1981)
Below: Bryan MacMahon (1909 – 1998)

CO-FOUNDERS OF IRISH PEN:

Bulmer Hobson
(1883 – 1969)

Frank Pakenham (1905 – 2001),
7th Earl of Longford (Lord Longford)

Seán Ó Faoláin (1900 – 1991)

COMMITTEE MEMBERS OF IRISH PEN:

Liam O'Flaherty
(1896 – 1984)

Below left:
Bryan Walter Guinness
(1905 – 1992), 2nd Baron
Moyne (Lord Moyne)

Below right: Barbara Walsh
(1932 –)

Annual PEN dinner at Nieve's Restaurant, Dalkey 1981. *Left to right:* Fr J. Anthony Gaughan, Gordon Thomas, Charles J. Haughey, TD, Sam McAughtry and Arthur Flynn

Annual PEN dinner at National Yacht Club, Dún Laoghaire, 1996. *Left to right:* Arthur Flynn, Margaret Neylon, O.Z. Whitehead, President Mary Robinson, Sheila Flitton, Fr J. Anthony Gaughan, Marita Conlon McKenna and Krzysztof Romanowski

Presentation of A.T. Cross/Irish PEN Literary Award at Royal St George Yacht Club, Dún Laoghaire, 1999.
Left to right: John B. Keane, President Mary McAleese

Presentation of the A.T. Cross/Irish PEN Literary Award at Royal St George Yacht Club, Dún Laoghaire in 2000.
Left to right: Brian Friel, Fr J. Anthony Gaughan, Séamus Heaney

Presentation of the A.T. Cross/Irish PEN Literary Award at the Royal St George Yacht Club, Dún Laoghaire, 2001.
Left to right: Paul Gibney (A.T. Cross), Edna O'Brien, President Mary McAleese, Arthur Flynn, Fr J. Anthony Gaughan, Mrs Nesta Tuomey

Presentation of the A.T. Cross/Irish PEN Literary Award at the Beaufield Mews Restaurant 2002.
Left to right: William Trevor, Maeve Binchy, Fr J. Anthony Gaughan, Gordon Snell

RECIPIENTS OF IRISH PEN AWARD:

Maeve Binchy (2002)　　John McGahern (2003)　　Neil Jordan (2004)

Séamus Heaney (2005)　　　　Jennifer Johnston (2006)

RECIPIENTS OF THE IRISH PEN AWARD:

Thomas Kilroy (2008)   Roddy Doyle (2009)   Brendan Kennelly (2010)

Joseph O'Connor (2012)

Colm Tobín (2011)

RECIPIENTS OF THE IRISH PEN AWARD:

John Banville (2013)

Frank McGuinness (2014)

Eilís Ní Dhuibhne (2015)

Anne Enright (2018

Writers' Week
1986.
Left to right:
Desmond
O'Malley, TD
and
Fr J. Anthony
Gaughan,
president of
Writers' Week

Bottom left to right: Gerry Adams, leader of the Republican movement; Albert Reynolds, Taoiseach; and John Hume, leader of the Social Democratic and Labour Party; meet in Dublin in 1994

Meeting in London to finalise arrangements for proposed 38th PEN International Congress in Dún Laoghaire in September 1971. *Front row, 3rd from left*: Judge Kenneth Deale (chairman, Irish PEN) *Back Row, 2nd from left*: Barbara Walsh (treasurer Irish PEN), *2nd from right*: Desmond Clarke (secretary, Irish PEN)

Heinrich Böll, president of PEN International who presided at the 38th Congress

Bottom following page:
Irish PEN Dinner 2018: *Left to right:* Catherine Dunne (recipient of
Irish PEN award 2019), Timmie Conway (treasurer, Irish PEN),
Anthony Glavin (Freedom to Write campaign), Lia Mills (Freedom to
Write campaign), Vanessa Fox-O'Loughlin (chair, Irish PEN)

Irish PEN Dinner 2018: *Left to right;* Liz McManus (Irish Writers Centre), Eilís Ní Dhuibhne (novelist), Fr J. Anthony Gaughan (President, Irish PEN), June Considine (Freedom to Write campaign), Josepha Madigan (minister for culture, heritage and the Gaeltacht)

Visit to Arás an Uachtaráin to launch the 'Word' 2018:
Left to right: Fr J. Anthony Gaughan (President, Irish PEN), Liz McManus
(Freedom to Write campaign), President Michael D. Higgins, June Considine
(Freedom to Write campaign)

The 84th PEN International Congress at Pune in India in October 2018 was attended by more than 400 writers from over 80 countries. Irish PEN was represented by Timmie Conway.
Left to right: Two delegates from South Korea, delegate from Wales PEN, Timmie Conway, third delegate from South Korea

Jennifer Clement, president of International PEN, who presided over the
84th Congress at Pune in India. From 2009 to 2012 Clement was president
of PEN Mexico, where her work was focussed on the disappearance and
killing of journalists

The venue for the dinner in November 1982 was the Mirabeau Restaurant, near Dún Laoghaire. The proprietor, Seán Kinsella, was a consummate publicist and scarcely a week passed without a report of a local or visiting celebrity dining in the restaurant. The cuisine, it seems, was excellent and the charges exorbitant! Not least because it was probable that a report of the dinner would appear in the press — as indeed it did — Kinsella agreed to provide the PEN dinner at a reasonable price, on condition that the price was not disclosed to anyone. The dinner was excellent and, in his chef's attire, Kinsella welcomed each guest as he or she arrived.

Colm Ó Briain, who had only recently been appointed to take charge of the Arts Council, was the guest of honour. In an address which was directed more towards the press than his listeners he set out his plans for the future of the arts in the country. The volatile Dermot Morgan was the principal speaker. A short time earlier I had prepared him and his wife — a Lutheran girl from Hamburg — for their marriage. I reminded him that he owed me a good turn and he kindly agreed to be our principal speaker, even after I cautioned him that there would be no fee. (Years later he was the star in the wonderful show 'Fr Ted'. Like many others I was greatly saddened and shocked at his sudden and premature death in 1998.)

At that time Morgan was a teacher and was attempting to ease into the entertainment business. He appeared frequently from the audience in Gay Byrne's *The Late, Late Show*. He would either do a take on Fr Brian D'Arcy, CP, as 'Fr Trendy', or as a Gaelic League, hurley-wielding troglodyte. In introducing Morgan I attempted to be amusing. Among my remarks I joked that he was with us 'at enormous expense' and I made references to his 'Fr Trendy' and 'Seán, the Gaelic Leaguer and GAA enthusiast'. Morgan did not disappoint and, complete with his hurley, was very entertaining with his routine on the hurley-wielder. However, when he sat down he was furious. He accused me of lying about his fee and pointed out that no entertainer or author wishes to be type-cast! Unfortunately I did not improve his mood by suggesting that it was time he grew up.

I had a similar experience on one other occasion. In 1986, as president of Writers' Week, it was my responsibility to introduce Desmond O'Malley, TD, and invite him to open the festival. During the previous weeks he had been touring the country, urging support for the newly established Progressive Democrats, of which he was a co-founder and leader. His efforts and those of his colleagues had received extraordinarily generous coverage in the media. To lighten my preliminary remarks, I said I was privileged to introduce a person some of those present might have heard of. When O'Malley sat down after an effective pitch for his new party, he told me he did not appreciate my brand of humour.

The amiable and unassuming President Patrick J. Hillery and his wife, Maeve, honoured the annual dinner in 1983. The then-promising playwright, Bernard Farrell, was the principal speaker. In the following year Richard Burke, a newly-appointed EEC Commissioner, in his grand manner shared with us his vision of the Europe of the future. The guest of honour in 1985 was Cardinal Tomás Ó Fiaich; the principal speaker was Ciaran Carty who after years as literary editor of the *Sunday Independent* had become arts editor of the recently-launched *Sunday Tribune*. The committee was particularly appreciative of the cardinal's presence. Already that day he had attended three public functions and in the small hours intended with his driver to return to Armagh city through the so-called bandit country of South Armagh.

The cardinal was at his jovial best. When I introduced him to Gordon Thomas, the latter invited both of us for lunch during the following week at his residence near Ashford. The cardinal regretted that he would not be free to accept the invitation, but Thomas made me promise that I would. In due course I enjoyed a lunch and pleasant afternoon with him and his German wife. The top-selling author showed me around the re-furbished old rectory, which had an indoor swimming-pool. He had a number of research-assistants and his study was packed with files. On the wall were clocks indicating all the time-zones of the world! I got the impression that Thomas lived his life halfway between the world of reality and that of imagination. But then that seems to be true of some celebrity creators of fiction.

The guest of honour in 1986 was Seán MacBride. For his work under the aegis of the UN for justice and peace in South West Africa he had been awarded the international Lenin Peace Prize and the Nobel Peace Prize. In his strange guttural accent he spoke about the danger of a nuclear holocaust, decried the arms race in which the two superpowers were engaged and urged writers, including members of PEN, to champion, and also be active in, peace and anti-nuclear-power movements.

In the following year Mrs Margaret Heckler, the new US ambassador, was the chief guest. She was jovial, outgoing and a fine speaker. A leading member of the Republican Party, she had had responsibility for education in President Ronald Reagan's first administration and was known to have been one of his close confidants.

As some politicians are prone to do, she spoke at some length. This was in sharp contrast to Francis Stuart, another special guest. He was not at all comfortable when addressing an audience and spoke very briefly. A very large person, and quietly-spoken, he did not even enjoy being in a crowd. However, he was most engaging when one talked to him face-to-face. This I had learnt at University Church, when I prepared the papers for his third marriage after the death of his second wife. By a curious coincidence his first marriage in 1920 to Iseult, daughter of Maud Gonne, also took place in University Church. He told me it was a rather furtive ceremony, as at that time he was 'on the run' from the crown forces.

Our principal speaker was Conor Brady, the distinguished journalist, who spoke about his profession. A newspaper, he said, could have a number of co-existing roles. It could aim at entertaining and bringing fun into the lives of its readers. Or, as he stated in words attributed to the legendary newspaperman, H.L. Mencken, it could set out to comfort the afflicted and afflict the comfortable.

But for him the purpose of a good newspaper in society was twofold, namely, to allow that society to hold a mirror to itself and to give it a window on the wider world. These objectives, he insisted, were achieved by combining reporting which was factually based with commentary and analysis. The latter included subjective judgment which, he acknowledged, may not always be sound. Conor concluded by raising a flag for his own newspaper, the *Irish Times*. He pointed out it had a long tradition of sending Irish journalists to report the wider world rather than simply relying on agency or wire reports, which inevitably were filtered through the eyes of British, US or European correspondents.

The British ambassador, Nicholas Fenn (later Sir Nicholas Fenn) and his wife, Susan, honoured the annual dinner in 1988. The actor, Alan Stanford, gave the best address I heard at any of our dinners. For me it was a most enjoyable occasion. Both the ambassador and his wife were born and raised in a manse, knew as much as I did about clerical life and were delightful company

A year later I received a message from the British embassy enquiring if I would be free to accept an invitation to a dinner party about a week later. I replied in the affirmative and was told it would be at Le Coq Hardi. As I had never heard of this restaurant, I had to check it out in the telephone directory. It was a family-run concern and when I arrived in the evening of the dinner I was warmly greeted by them. They were parishioners of Mount Merrion and knew me when I had served there.

It seems the dinner was in honour of a senior foreign

office official, whose role was to visit (and, I suppose, inspect) embassies around the world. The other guests were: Stephen Collins, the distinguished political journalist; Professor Ronan Fanning, history department, UCD; John FitzGerald, of the Economic and Social Research Institute; and Gerard Hogan, a lecturer in the law department, TCD. I was intrigued by the menu; the wine list was equally interesting. There were over a dozen dishes on offer. I noted the name of different kinds of food which I had not come across since reading Shakespeare's plays at college. The prices were extraordinary. I mumbled that they seemed to be excessive. Susan Fenn heard me and said in a tone heard by all: 'Fr Tony, don't be worried about the price. Just remember Margaret Thatcher is paying for all this'.

The man from the foreign office had a remarkable story to tell. He gave a riveting account of witnessing the fall of the Berlin Wall. A week earlier he happened to be in the British consulate in Berlin. On the late television news Berliners were to be seen pulling down parts of the Wall. This followed a confused statement, issued earlier, to the effect that the East German border police were not to be deployed to protect it. Like thousands of others, some in their night clothes, he went to witness for himself this historic event.

The official from the foreign office was very calm and self-assured. He was also pencil-thin and athletic-looking. I was not surprised by this feature. At this dinner in his honour, he ordered a large eating-apple and a small knife and spent the time slowly eating the apple, while the rest of us tucked into a Lucullan feast.

There was very little small talk at the dinner. The first topic of discussion was the prospect of the reunification of Germany. Helmut Kohl, the German chancellor, had developed a very positive relationship with Mikhail Gorbachev, leader of the Soviet Union, and did not find him unduly disposed to block German reunification. The other war allies: US, Great Britain and France were divided on the issue. The US and France were supportive of Kohl's determination to achieve German reunification as soon as possible. However, Prime Minister Thatcher and her government were highlighting all kinds of reasons for delaying it, not least that the safety of Europe depended on a weak and divided Germany.

The British diplomats scarcely intervened in the general discussion. On the one hand, Stephen Collins and I argued that the best course of action was the rapid and peaceful reunification of Germany. This would eliminate further potential causes of conflict and would mercifully draw a line under the appalling events of the previous fifty years. On the other hand, the other guests approached the issue, it seemed to me, mainly from a British geo-political perspective. I was also surprised at how cautious they were in expressing their opinions and their general deference, an attitude, I hasten to add, in no way encouraged by the ambassador.

Inevitably, the question of Northern Ireland arose. Here again Stephen Collins and I were at one, articulating an Irish nationalist point of view. The views of the others again seemed to me to have been heavily influenced by political correctness. Even the two-nations theory received an airing! I told the ambassador that as an Irish person I viewed Northern Ireland as Ireland's British problem not as Britain's Irish problem, that it was a political problem with religious overtones not a religious problem with political overtones, and that the only lasting solution to the difficulties was British withdrawal after a long period of justice, peace and reconciliation. Stephen Collins's view, I hasten to add, was far more nuanced and less stark than mine.

In 1989 our guest of honour was Alice Taylor. Then at the peak of her popularity, in person and on the page she was redolent of what Daniel Corkery termed 'The Hidden Ireland'. David Marcus was the principal speaker. Irish PEN was gratified in having an opportunity to acknowledge his sterling and selfless contribution to Irish writing and especially his encouragement of young aspiring writers, when he was literary editor of the *Irish Press*. I had my own reasons to be pleased. David, with a generous acknowledgement, had based *A land in flames* (1988), his third novel, on *Memoirs of Jeremiah Mee, RIC* which I had published in 1975 and was a much cherished friend.

In the years that followed John Banville, Maeve Binchy, Ernest Bryll (Polish ambassador and poet), Mrs Jean Kennedy Smith (US ambassador) and John Wilson (a senior member of a number of Irish governments), among others, enhanced the annual dinner. Archbishop Robin Eames was the guest of honour in 1997, with Niall Toíbín the principal speaker. Realising that the gathering was convivial rather than one at which serious matters were discussed the archbishop set aside his prepared script and gave as entertaining a stand-up, knock-about performance as I ever enjoyed. Niall Toíbín, on the other hand, was close to confirming the received wisdom about the personality of the comic. He was silent and morose. However, when he got to his feet, he was also immensely entertaining with his own distinctive, laconic and dead-pan humour.

President Mary Robinson, the first woman to be president of Ireland, honoured the annual dinner in 1996. From the outset there was considerable emphasis on protocol and during the entire proceedings she did not seem to be relaxed. Much of her conversation with me was about the manner in which she was 'invigorating' the countryside by visiting and encouraging local communities, a role for which at that time she was receiving justifiable acclaim.

In her address she spoke about human rights and the plight of Ken Saro-Wiwa. He was at the centre of a struggle in the oil-rich province of Ogoni land in Nigeria, where people were attempting to defend their individual rights and their tribal rights against encroachment by multinational oil companies, backed by the federal military government. She did not, however, refer to what for me was the most important and basic right of all, the general right to life. Yet just over six months later she was appointed UN High Commissioner for Human Rights!

President Mary McAleese was the guest of honour in 1999 and 2001. There was a minimum of fuss about protocol and she manifestly enjoyed meeting as many people as she could. A person of high intelligence, she spoke interestingly and courageously on almost any topic. She and her husband, Martin, were excellent company and were rated by the committee the most popular guests at our annual dinner over many years.

I was delighted to have the opportunity to spend time talking to Mrs McAleese, about whom I had already formed a high opinion. I had met her in 1986 when she launched *The facilitators* by Doris Manly and others. For the most part, this was an honest, courageous and well-argued account of how facilitators were being used consciously and unconsciously to promote the secularist agenda in all areas of life in Ireland. Her encouragement of the authors of the book ran counter to the prevailing ethos of the time. I met her again in 1996 when she chaired the inaugural lecture at the Eighth Desmond Greaves Summer School which is sponsored by the Irish Labour History Society. The topic was the then much-criticised 1937 Constitution. She recalled vividly her experience of seeing her home and those of Catholic neighbours in north Belfast being burnt by a hostile mob, with the tacit collusion of elements of the security forces. At such a time she pointed out one envied countries which had a written Constitution, guaranteeing the rights of every citizen.

It is sometimes stated that writers tend not to be sociable. I have never had evidence of this down through the years. I have found writers, almost without exception, and especially my colleagues on the Irish PEN committee, to be most congenial. And I recall with pleasure expatriates who from time to time served on the committee: Morgan Llywelyn (novelist); Anne McCaffrey (science fiction writer); O.Z.Whitehead (biographer) from the US; Pat Connole from Australia; Ian St James (novelist) from Britain; and Krzysztof Joseph and Maria Romanowski (translators) from Poland.

Ian St James was the pseudonym under which Don Taylor wrote. He had served in the British army and later resided as an expatriate writer in a number of 'Britain's trouble spots'. I suspected that his was a role in Ireland similar to that of John Betjeman (the future poet laureate) during World War II.

O.Z. Whitehead, member of the PEN committee from 1983 until he died in 1998, was, perhaps, the most popular member to serve on it. Zebbie, as we called him, was born in New York in 1911. He had a passion for the theatre and delighted in acting professionally up to a few years before he died. He played secondary roles in a number of the most highly-acclaimed films produced at Hollywood and elsewhere in the 1930s, 1940s, 1950s and 1960s. His most memorable role was as 'Al' in John Ford's 1940 film version of John Steinbeck's *The Grapes of Wrath*. He knew many of the outstanding actors and actresses of that era and was a close friend of Lillian and Dorothy Gish, and of Katherine Hepburn, about whom he enjoyed telling numerous anecdotes. Zebbie's other great passion was the Baha'i Faith, of which he became a member in 1950 and a leading personality from the 1960s onwards. Apart from an important memoir on Lillian Gish, his writing was on various aspects of the Baha'i Faith. His practice of his faith was edifying and in accordance with it he never lost an opportunity to champion and promote the highest standards and values in every area of personal and social behaviour.

CHAPTER FOUR

Irish PEN in the New Millennium

ITH THE ADVENT of the millennium Irish PEN renewed its commitment to the aims of PEN. These included a concern for the craft of writing and a dedication to the defence of freedom of expression and the promotion of international good-will. The Centre had 87 members and 77 associate members and the committee continued to organise its usual annual programme. This featured the monthly meeting followed by a lecture, panel discussion, a reading or a talk. The annual dinner and presentation of the Irish PEN/A.T. Cross Award for Literature at the Royal St George Yacht Club also continued and on most occasions the Centre was represented at the International PEN Congress.

The monthly programme in 2006 was fairly typical. In January the Irish PEN dinner was held in the Royal St George Yacht Club with Jennifer Johnston the winner of the Irish PEN/A.T. Cross Award. In February 'Romance Night' was chaired by Kathleen Sheehan-O'Connor, as authors Claudia Carroll, Denise Deegan and Sarah Webb entertained the attendance with their insights into writing the modern novel. In March Patricia O'Reilly (author), Michael O'Brien (publisher) and Fr Tony Gaughan (author) provided an informative overview of the world of non-fiction and the opportunities to publish in this area. In April 'Dublin – A Writer's City' was sponsored by The Dublin City Arts Office and was chaired by Lia Mills. Authors Dermot Bolger, Philip Casey, Christine Dwyer Hickey and Peter Sheridan read from their work and talked about the city and its influences on their writing.

In May the annual general meeting was held. In October Marita Conlon-McKenna chaired a panel discussion on 'How to be Published'. In November Fr Tony Gaughan described the challenges and joys involved in compiling local history. In December Evan Boland, professor of humanities at Standford University, California, and director of its creative writing programme, read from her work and discussed her life as a poet.

Much of the correspondence received by the Centre from the International PEN office concerned the plight of writers – some who had been murdered, others tortured and imprisoned, and accounts of the oppression suffered by writers in countries with autocratic regimes of the right or the left. In the summer of 2003 Terry Carlbom, secretary of International PEN, visited Dublin. Arthur Flynn and I reported to him on the activities of the Irish Centre. Like many Swedes he spoke English perfectly. He expressed a keen interest in the major Irish literary figures and his wish to know more about them. Subsequently in an exchange of letters I provided him with a broad perspective of the then Irish literary scene.

The annual dinner and presentation of the Irish Pen Award continued to be the Centre's social highlight. Brian

Friel received the award in 2000. It was presented by his friend Séamus Heaney. At the dinner I greatly appreciated the privilege of sitting between those two outstanding literati of our time – the poet Heaney and the playwright Friel - and I enjoyed their congenial company and lively conversation.

The flamboyant and somewhat theatrical Edna O'Brien was the recipient in 2001. It was presented by President Mary McAleese, our guest of honour. It was the second time we had Mrs McAleese as our guest. She came to the dinner with just her driver and she was delightful company. In fact, her presence was the highlight of the occasion. She was a fascinating foil to Edna O'Brien who was full of affectation. That festive occasion was also greatly enhanced by David Norris, another extraordinary extrovert, who delivered a characteristically rambunctious after-dinner speech, replete with references to Joyce.

The award went to William Trevor in 2002. Author of twelve novels and numerous collections of short stories, he was one of Ireland's most internationally revered writers at that time. His friend, Maeve Binchy, who then also enjoyed a world reputation as a novelist, made the presentation. Maeve was accompanied by her husband Gordon Snell, a children's writer. While insisting that she was a hopeless public speaker, she entertained the gathering with a quirky and self-depreciating address.

There is a good reason why I vividly remember that annual dinner and presentation. It was held just a year prior to the invasion of Iraq by the US and its allies on 20 March 2003. For more than a year, the Western media outlets were ratcheting up popular support for that course of action which President George W. Bush had come to regard as a necessary crusade. I was deeply convinced that such an intervention would have disastrous consequences and I had expressed as much in a letter published in the press. When I rose to welcome the guests to the dinner and invite Maeve Binchy to make the presentation I strongly argued against the proposed invasion. There was a mixed reaction from those present, most of them disagreeing with my stand. As for Maeve, she glared at me! I did not know then that Barbara Bush, mother of President George W. Bush, was one of Maeve's most devoted fans and that they had formed a firm friendship. In the event, with regard to the invasion, while prior to it everybody seemed to favour it, subsequently it proved to be a catastrophic blunder on a geo-political scale.

John McGahern was the recipient of the award in 2003 and the guest of honour who presented it was John O'Donoghue, minister for arts, sport and tourism. McGahern, a master of understatement, I found to be very amiable and I enjoyed immensely my chat with him during the dinner. Neil Jordan was the recipient in 2004. He had arrived in Dublin airport from Los Angeles just three hours earlier. Because of the jet lag and a few extra libations he was not at his articulate best when he rose to acknowledge the award.

The Nobel Laureate Séamus Heaney received the award in 2005. It was presented by his friend Brian Friel. This was a reversal of their roles at the dinner in 2000. I was delighted to renew my acquaintance with these two distinguished litterateurs. Both were as amiable as ever and made time to have a word with many of the attendees, some of whom had brought books to have them signed by Heaney.

Jennifer Johnston, the playwright, was the recipient in 2006. It was presented by Roddy Doyle who enhanced the occasion with a witty and entertaining address. The recipient in 2007 was Maeve Binchy. Declan Kiberd, head of the English department in UCD, in presenting the award, provided a thoughtful appraisal of her work to date. Thomas Kilroy, best known for his novel *The Big Chapel*, was the winner of the award in 2008 and it was presented by Jennifer Johnston. In 2009 it was Roddy Doyle's turn to receive the award and it was presented to him by Fintan O'Toole, who expressed his pleasure in doing so 'as a friend and fellow-Northsider'!

Brendan Kennelly was the recipient in 2010. He entertained the gathering with a recital of some of his most popular poetry. During the dinner I enjoyed reminiscing about our experiences playing football in North Kerry. Colm Tóibín received the award in 2011. In presenting it Mary Clarke, director of the Arts Council, provided a superb appraisal of his work up to that time.

President Michael D. Higgins was the guest of honour in 2012 and presented the award to Joseph O'Connor. From that year onwards, a chair has been placed in a prominent position at the annual dinner with a sign on it indicating that it had been reserved for the 'Imprisoned Writer'! With a nod towards the empty chair the president made a spirited appeal for everyone to be actively interested in and to always champion freedom of expression, human rights and egalitarianism. The brilliant and prolific John Banville received the award in 2013. Known to be taciturn, he lived up to his reputation on the night but he exuded friendliness in his own way and he was an interesting foil to the gregarious Jimmy Deenihan, minister for arts, heritage and the Gaeltacht, who presented the award.

Frank McGuinness, best known for his *Observe the Sons of Ulster Marching Towards the Somme* and for his translation and adaptation of literary classics, won the award in 2013. It was presented by his friend and fellow-playwright, Sebastian Barry. McGuinness, head of the English department at UCD, was joined at the dinner by many of his academic colleagues. I was delighted to renew my acquaintance with one of them, Anthony Roche, who had just recently retired from the chair of English in the college. He reminded me that I had trained him to be an altar-server in Monkstown, where his family resided and I served as a curate in the 1970s.

The next two winners were novelists Eilís Ní Dhuibhne in 2015 and Anne Enright in 2018. Eilís, who published work in Irish and English, acknowledged the award in the native tongue as well as in English. The much-acclaimed Anne Enright, winner of the Brooker Prize and many others besides, was characteristically succinct in her acceptance speech. June Considine, who made the presentation in the unavoidable absence of prolific playwright Bernard Farrell, amply made up for the deficit.

Catherine Dunne received the award in 2019. A prolific

novelist, she won the Boccaccio International Prize for *The things we know now* in 2013. The PEN award was presented by Josepha Madigan, minister for culture, heritage and the Gaeltacht. In responding, Catherine recalled the odyssey she had travelled as a writer of fiction and non-fiction. June Considine provided an account of the 'Freedom to Write campaign' and collected signatures for a protest to be presented to the Turkish government with regard to the torture and imprisonment of a journalist who had criticised misconduct by the Turkish army. And Lia Mills presented a heart-felt account of Catherine as a friend, writer and fellow community activist.

With Kay Boland I attended the International Pen Congress in Belgrade in 2011. It was held in the shadow of the internecine conflict which followed the break-up of the federation that was Yugoslavia. It was clear that the Serbian government was using the event to signal its determination to chart a new course with regard to its closest neighbours and the wider world. On one of the outings in Belgrade visitors were shown a huge crater in the midst of a built-up area. It had been the site of the headquarters of the Serbian army and had been 'taken out' by a US missile with the finesse of a surgeon's scalpel. The government had made no effort to clear the site, leaving it, it seems, as a warning to an extreme nationalist element in Serbian society not to consider re-opening the Balkan conflict.

I attended the 78th International Pen Congress in Gyeongju, South Korea, in 2012. The country had already hosted a Congress in Soul in 1970. The theme of the

Congress, appropriately enough was 'Literature, Media and Human Rights'. Superbly organised, it was sponsored by the ministry of culture, sports and tourism. From the lavish support the government provided to the Congress it was clear that it regarded it as a wonderful opportunity to showcase the almost miraculous transition of the country from the devastation of war to becoming one of the most affluent and industrialised countries in the world. One of the ancillary outings was a blatant public-relations exercise. It was a visit to a site where a massive nuclear-power station was under construction. This was generating considerable controversy at that time and local journalists and the visitors were left in no doubt by the tour guides with regard to the safety and merits of nuclear power.

The Congress in South Korea followed the pattern of such gatherings. There were the key-note addresses. The first involved welcoming the visitors. In the second Nigerian Wole Soyinka, winner of the Nobel Prize in 1986, underlined the importance of not only freedom of expression but also of independent and unregimented thought. In the third Jean-Marie Gustave Le Clézio from France, winner of the Nobel Prize in 2006, argued that the new media do not compete with the old ones, rather they bring to them a new existence and are 'a good omen for democracy and peace'.

A poet who had escaped from North Korea, described the appalling socio-economic situation in his homeland, where just recently a food shortage had led to the death of three million people. He went on to outline the brutal suppression of writers in the communist country. And a play by another escapee outlined the horrors inflicted on the inmates of that country's multiple prison-camps.

Since 1984 International PEN has organised an annual conference on 'Writers for Peace' at Bled in Slovenia. With the Irish Centre's treasurer, Timmy Conway, a one-time Labour Party Senator and former treasurer of the Party, I attended the conference in 2015. I found it memorable for three reasons. First at all the sessions there was a routine shouting match between those from Israeli PEN and the PEN representatives from Palestine. Second, the immensely patient director and chair of all those sessions was a Franciscan. He was a theologian who lectured at the order's Slovenian major seminary for one half of the year and at their Pontifical University of St Anthony in Rome in the other half. Finally, there was Timmy's popularity with all the attendees, owing to his infectious sociability and readiness to lead and join in a sing-song.

I ended my twenty-five-year stint in the chair of Irish PEN in 2005, being succeeded by Marita Conlon-McKenna. An acclaimed writer for children, she was beginning her career as a novelist. She was succeeded by Catherine Daly, another novelist. Joe Armstrong, who was later a leading figure in the Humanist Association of Ireland, was in the chair for 2011 – 2012. Vanessa Fox-O'Loughlin, literary scout, founder of the Inkwell Group (a forum for assisting aspiring authors) and a successful novelist, has been in the chair since 2014.

I was elected president of Irish PEN in 2017, following the death of Brian Friel in 2015. A few years earlier the committee had generously honoured me with honorary life membership. Curiously, I was the fourth person from Listowel and its vicinity to be president of Irish PEN. The others were John B Keane (1928 - 2002), Bryan MacMahon (1909 – 98) and Maurice Walsh (1879 – 1964). While Keane and MacMahon were well-known, the shy and self-effacing Maurice Walsh was much less so. Yet he was a writer of considerable stature. Native of Ballydonoghue, he was educated at Lisselton national school and St Michael's College, Listowel. He entered the British civil service and was appointed to the excise department in Scotland. When the Irish Free State was established in 1922 he returned home to build up the customs and excise service of the new State. His first novel, *The Key above the Door,* appeared in 1923 and established him as a story-teller of the first rank. Subsequently he wrote twenty novels and numerous short stories. The Hollywood Academy Award winning film *The Quiet Man* was based on one of his stories. And his novel *Trouble in the Glen* was filmed in England in 1954.

In recent years, except in the case of a charismatic public figure, it has been difficult to attract a significant attendance to a monthly talk. Even panel discussions have been poorly attended. Hence Vanessa Fox-O'Loughlin, the current chair, has been prompted to nudge the Centre in a new direction. There is a new emphasis on initiatives to assist imprisoned writers. This has been spearheaded by Frank Geary, a former staff member in PEN's head office in London. The Centre has also joined with other groups of writers, such as the Front Line Defenders, the Freedom to Write campaign and others in promoting human rights and egalitarianism.

The present state and range of activity of Irish PEN is best summed-up in the 'Irish PEN Newsletter' of January 2019 prepared by the membership secretary, Pádraig Hanratty (see appendix 5). In the meantime, the Centre, one of the oldest in the world-wide PEN movement, is looking forward to participating in the centenary celebrations in London in 2021.

People come to PEN from widely different perspectives but all are at one in their lively and practical interest in the written word and their conviction with regard to the importance of freedom of expression. Serving on the committee as I have for almost forty-three years has given me the wonderful opportunity of working with generous and talented persons (see appendix 4). I have been greatly enriched by their friendship for which I am immensely grateful.

Report on 66th World Congress of PEN International

THE 66TH WORLD CONGRESS was held in the University of Warsaw in June 1999. Delegates from more than 70 countries attended. With Krzysztof Joseph and Maria Romanowski, two other members of our executive committee, I represented Irish PEN.

The theme of the Congress was 'Farewell to the 20th Century'. The unparalleled scientific and technological progress achieved throughout the century, the fall of empires, the end of colonialism, clear gains for women's rights and people becoming more equal — all tend to be over-looked when one reflects on the horrors associated with the century. One need but recall the slaughter in World War I, the Gulags, the Holocaust, the nuclear torching of the populations of Hiroshima and Nagasaki and the ethnic cleansing in Rwanda and the Balkan conflicts. In Warsaw, razed to the ground in November 1944 at the whim of a maniac, and in Poland, over which the greatest wars of the recent past raged and where the Holocaust was perpetrated by the Nazis, one could not but be acutely aware of those horrors. Few of those who contributed to the various discussions failed to refer to these unhappy aspects of the 20th century. Great stress was laid on the challenge to writers to ensure that in these instances at least history did not repeat itself.

Other challenges set out for the writer on the threshold of the 21st century and the new millennium were the need to encourage people to oppose totalitarianism and dictatorship and to caution people against the danger of abandoning a sense of community and becoming mere lonely inhabitants in the global village. The need for humans to respect nature was highlighted as was the importance of ensuring that science was the servant of man not man the servant of science.

Somewhat idealistically it was proposed that the manner in which writers could successfully face such challenges was by the unqualified pursuit of truth. This seeking of truth, it was stressed, was not to be deflected by ideological agendas. Nor was it to be frustrated by censorship.

Another issue which attracted the attention of congress was the dumbing-down of culture in general and literature in particular by present-day commercialism. In a paper on the subject Ronald Harwood of English PEN acknowledged the manner in which technology and the media had facilitated unprecedented access to cultural activities of all kinds. However, he detailed how the pressure of the market-place caused publishers and editors to ignore literature of the highest quality and to promote the banal and the kitsch. He urged writers to challenge this development but was not able to offer any specific advice on how the trend could be reversed.

Other important meetings were included under the umbrella of congress such as those convened by a Writers for Peace Committee and Women Writers' Committee. Strong support was given to a Universal Declaration of Linguistic Rights by the Translation and Linguistic Rights Committee. At Congress there was a seminar organised by UNESCO on 'The Role of International Writers Organisations' in the 20th Century and their association with UNESCO'.

Writers in prison were not forgotten. At a press conference a detailed case-list of fellow-writers in prison, those who had been tortured and those who had been murdered, was provided. For the most part they were citizens of the remaining Communist-controlled countries: China, Cuba, North Korea and Vietnam. But other countries such as Iran, Iraq, Mexico, Myanmar (Burma) and Turkey also had their complement of prisoners of conscience!

The Congress at plenary and subordinate sessions emphasised the importance it attached to this aspect of PEN's activities. Professor DoanViet Hoat of the Buddhist University of Ho Chi Minh city, who was released in September 1998 mid-way through an 18-year prison sentence largely owing to lobbying by Polish PEN, was the chief guest of honour at congress. And a monograph circulated to those attending the congress indicated how dangerous it can be in some parts of the world to speak or write the truth. It carried on its front cover an appreciation of Slavko Curuvija, editor of several independent newspapers, and a detailed account of the background to his assassination in Belgrade on 11 April 1999.

Rules of Irish PEN
Compiled by Judge Kenneth Deale

NAME AND OBJECTS OF PEN

1. The association shall be called PEN (i.e. Poets, Playwrights, Editors, Essayists, Novelists). Translators shall be eligible as members. The Association exists to promote the friendly co-operation of writers in every country in the interests of literature, freedom of expression and international goodwill.

QUALIFICATION FOR MEMBERSHIP

2. The qualification for membership shall be recognized standing in the literary world. The committee shall be the final judge of the qualification of any candidate for election. Members shall be required to subscribe to the principles laid down in the PEN charter, as passed at the international congress held in Copenhagen in 1948, viz:
PEN affirms that:

(1) Literature, national though it be in origin, knows no frontiers, and should remain common currency between nations in spite of political or international upheavals.

(2) In all circumstances, and particularly in time of

war, works of art, the patrimony of humanity at large, should be left untouched by national or political passion.

(3) Members of PEN should at all times use what influence they have in favour of good understanding and mutual respect between nations; they pledge themselves to do their utmost to dispel race, class and national hatreds and to champion the ideal of one humanity living in peace in one world.

(4) PEN stands for the principle of unhampered transmission of thought within each nation and between all nations, and members pledge themselves to oppose any form of suppression of freedom of expression in the country and community to which they belong. PEN declares for a free press and opposes arbitrary censorship in time of peace. It believes that the necessary advance of the world towards a more highly organised political and economic order renders a free criticism of governments, administrations and institutions imperative. And since freedom implies voluntary restraint, members pledge themselves to oppose such evils of a free press as mendacious publication, deliberate falsehood and distortion of facts for political and personal ends.

Membership of PEN is open to all qualified writers, editors and translators who subscribe to these aims, without regard to nationality, race, colour or religion.

SUBSCRIPTIONS

3. Members shall pay such subscription as shall be decided at an annual general meeting.

PAYMENT OF SUBSCRIPTIONS

4. The annual subscription shall become due on the 1st January in each year or on any other date which shall be determined from time to time.

ELECTION OF MEMBERS

5 (a) The name, permanent address and qualifications of every candidate for membership shall be entered on the application form.

   The candidate must be proposed and seconded by two members of the Centre both of whom, preferably, he or she should be personally known and both of whom should be familiar with his or her works; both these sponsors must sign the application form and shall — if required by the committee — produce evidence in writing of qualifications.

   Every candidate shall be elected by a majority vote at a committee meeting and the decision of such majority shall be final. A candidate having failed to secure election at a committee meeting shall not be eligible to be proposed for election again until the expiration of six months.

   (b) Temporary membership may be granted to visiting writers, editors or translators from other countries during the period of their residence in this country.

HONORARY MEMBERS

6. The committee may invite to be members of honour such persons as they shall think fit.

COMMITTEE – NUMBER AND CONSTITUTION

7. The management of the Centre is vested in a committee consisting of the chairman, the vice-chairman, the honorary secretary and the honorary treasurer (who shall be ex-officio members), and such other members of the Centre as the committee may decide.

    Five members of the committee shall form a quorum. The committee shall have power to fill any vacancies in their number.

ELECTION OF COMMITTEE

8 (a) Four members of the outgoing committee shall be elected by the committee prior to the annual general meeting, to serve on the incoming committee.

(b) The officers and remaining members of the committee shall be elected at the annual general meeting.

CASTING VOTE

9. In all cases of the committee coming to a division, if the numbers be equal, the chairman, in addition to his vote as a member of the committee shall have a casting vote.

SUB-COMMITTEES

10. The committee shall have power to elect sub-committees.

ANNUAL GENERAL MEETING

11. The date of the annual general meeting and of any other meetings shall be fixed by the committee.

REPORT AT ANNUAL GENERAL MEETING

12. An abstract of the audited accounts for the past year shall be available at the annual general meeting.

ALTERATION OF RULES

13. At the annual general meeting any motion for the alteration of the rules or otherwise affecting the interests of PEN may be brought forward by any member; but no such motion shall be made unless seven days' notice has been given by sending a copy of the motion to the honorary secretary.

LIABILITY OF MEMBERS

14. The liability of the committee and members shall be limited to the amount of their subscriptions, and any rights which a member may have in PEN shall be determined to have ended when his membership ceases.

MEMBERSHIP

15. Membership of one Centre constitutes membership of all.

ASSOCIATE MEMBERS

16. The committee may elect associate members.

Consultative Council of Irish PEN. The Consultative Council of Irish PEN was formed in 1954 at the unanimous wish of both the Belfast and Dublin Centres. The Council consists of four members from the Belfast Centre and four members from the Dublin Centre as appointed by the committee of each Centre. The Council meets at intervals in either Belfast or Dublin to discuss matters of mutual interest or matters on which joint action is deemed desirable and to elect annually a president of Irish PEN. (This Council no longer exists since the Belfast Centre closed down in 1977.)

The Charter of International PEN

INTRODUCTION

International PEN is a worldwide association of writers. A leading voice of literature, PEN brings together poets, novelists, essayists, historians, playwrights, critics, translators, editors, journalists, and screenwriters in a common concern for the craft and art of writing and a commitment to freedom of expression through the written word. Through its 149 Centres in more than 100 countries, PEN operates on all six continents.

Founded in London in1921 by novelist Catherine Amy Dawson Scott, PEN originally stood for Poets, Essayists, Editors and Novelists, but now membership is open to all qualified writers who subscribe to the PEN charter. Its founding and early members included among others, Joseph Conrad, D.H. Lawrence, George Bernard Shaw, and John Galsworthy.

Through its meetings and Congresses, PEN offers a forum where writers meet freely to discuss their work and to speak out for writers silenced in their own countries. Through the programmes of its individual Centres and through its international committees – including the Writers in Prison Committee, the Writers for Peace Committee, the Women Writers Committee, the Committee for Translation and Linguistic Rights – PEN works to promote friendship and goodwill among writers, to foster understanding through literature, to dispel class, race and national hatreds. It upholds freedom of expression and defends writers suffering from oppressive regimes, be they regimes of the extreme right or extreme left.

In recent years International PEN Congresses have been hosted by PEN Centres in Venezuela, Japan, the United States, Germany, Switzerland, Puerto Rico, South Korea, Holland, Canada, Portugal, Austria, Catalonia, Spain, Brazil, Croatia, Czech Republic, Australia, Mexico, Scotland, Finland, Poland and Russia.

International PEN is governed by its Assembly of Delegates from each Centre which elects the officers and Executive Committee. The individual centres of PEN are self-governed. PEN is a non-political, non-governmental organization with consultative status at the United Nations and in formal relations with UNESCO.

The PEN Charter is based on resolutions passed at its International Congresses and may be summarised as follows.

PEN affirms that:

Literature, national though it be in origin, knows no frontiers, and should remain common currency between nations in spite of political or international upheavals.

In all circumstances, and particularly in time of war, works of art, the patrimony of humanity at large, should be left untouched by national or political passion.

Members of PEN should at all times use what influence they have in favour of good understanding and mutual respect between nations; they pledge themselves to do their utmost to dispel race, class and national hatreds, and to champion the ideal of one humanity living in peace in one world.

PEN stands for the principle of unhampered transmission of thought within each nation and between all nations, and members pledge themselves to oppose any form of suppression of freedom of expression in the country and community to which they belong, as well as throughout the world wherever this is possible. PEN declares for a free press and opposes arbitrary censorship in time of peace. It believes that the necessary advance of the world towards a more highly organised political and economic order renders a free criticism of governments, administrations and institutions imperative. And since freedom implies voluntary restraint, members pledge themselves to oppose such evils of a free press as mendacious publication, deliberate falsehood and distortion of facts for political and personal ends.

Membership of PEN is open to all qualified writers, editors and translators who subscribe to these aims, without regards to nationality, language, race, colour or religion.

Executive Committee of Irish PEN
2001 - 2002

President:	John B. Keane	(writer and playwright)
Life Member:	Séamus Heaney	(poet and Nobel Laureate)
Chairman:	Very Reverend Dr J.Anthony Gaughan	(writer and historian)
Secretary:	Arthur Flynn	(writer)
Treasurer:	Mrs Nesta Tuomey	(novelist)
Members:		
	Mrs Marita Conlon-McKenna	(novelist)
	Mrs Christine Dwyer Hickey	(novelist)
	Mrs Sheila Flitton	(actress and novelist)
	James Maher	(biographer)
	Mrs Patricia O'Reilly	(writer and novelist)
	Krzysztof Joseph Romanowski	(translator)
	Dr Maria Romanowski	(translator)
	Mrs Kathleen Sheehan O'Connor	(novelist)

Irish PEN newsletter, January 2019

Irish PEN
Association of Irish Writers

January 2019

DEFENDING THE RIGHT OF WRITERS

Contact us:
vanessa@writing.ie

WELCOME TO THE IRISH PEN NEWSLETTER

2018 Irish PEN Award

We are delighted to announce that the 2018 Irish PEN Award for an Outstanding Contribution to Irish Literature will be given to Catherine Dunne. She is the author of ten published novels including *The Things We Know Now*, which won the Giovanni Boccaccio International Prize for Fiction (2013) and was shortlisted for the Irish Book Awards. *The Years That Followed* was long listed for the International Dublin Literary Award 2018.

The Award Dinner takes place on Friday, 22 February at 7:00pm at the Royal St. George Yacht Club, Dun Laoghaire. Book your ticket via www.irishpen.com

LOOKING BACK AT 2018

A Reception with President Higgins

President Higgins is the Patron of the Irish Writers Centre and he has put the promotion of creativity, critical thought and the careful use of language at the heart of his Presidency.

In March 2018, members of Irish PEN, Word and the Irish Writers Centre visited President Higgins launch of WORD and Irish PEN's initiative to support International PENs Freedom to Write Campaign.

Freedom of expression and solidarity among writers are at the heart of PEN. PEN started in the aftermath of World

War One bringing writers together to within and between recently warring nations. PEN quickly expressed this same solidarity by campaigning for freedom of expression for all writers and for individual writers who were silenced, harassed, imprisoned and murdered because they had the courage to write.

Freedom to Write Campaign Supports PEN International to Protest Murder of Maltese Journalist Daphne Caruana Galizia

A letter was published simultaneously in newspapers across the world on Monday 16th April 2018, six months after the murder of Maltese journalist Daphne Caruana Galizia. This action was co-ordinated by PEN International. As part of the Freedom to Write Campaign, Irish PEN and WORD were in full support of this initiative and gathered signatories. The letter appeared in The Irish Independent on 16th April.

"We write to you on the six-month anniversary of the brutal assassination of our colleague, Daphne Caruana Galizia, Malta's foremost investigative journalist, to express our profound concern with developments in Malta in the context of the investigation into her assassination, and in particular regarding the behaviour of the management of Valletta 2018, the European Capital of Culture."

Daphne Caruana Galizia vigil and documentary

A recent vigil for Daphne took place in London and was attended by WORD and Irish PEN member Lia Mills. The candlelight vigil was held in the courtyard of St James's Church

opposite the Maltese High Commission.

Who Was Daphne and Why Was She Murdered is a recent documentary about Daphne Caruana Galizia. Irish PEN is looking in to the possibility of screening this thought-provoking documentary at a PEN evening in 2019. We'll keep you posted once details have been finalized.

84th PEN International Congress

Report from Timothy Conway

"The 84th PEN INTERNATIONAL CONGRESS was held in Pune, India in September. The Congress marked the 150th anniversary of the birth of the great Mahatma Gandhi. It was an extraordinary congress and PEN called upon the Indian government to act to protect freedom of expression.

"We received reports of the many writers that have been murdered, such as Malta's foremost investigative journalist, Daphne Caruana Galizia. PEN International's global membership of writers continue to reiterate our call for an independent, impartial and effective investigation into her killing.

"We remembered the murder of the reporter Marie Colvin who was about to report how a tiny baby had died that day because there was no medicine, how civilians, cold and terrified, were being targeted by President Assad's Military. The people of Homs in Syria, she said, felt the world had forsaken them.

"We remembered the campaign on the 15th November 2017 engaged writers to write letters of solidarity to our focus cases in Honduras, Equatorial Guinea, Syria. The campaign received wide-spread coverage. Ai Wiewei's letter to Zehra Dogan went viral in Turkey. We reached over 12.7 million people on social media.

"At the Lviv Congress, The Women's Manifesto was approved unanimously. The international campaign around the manifesto was launched on International woman's day 8 March 2018. The Manifesto has been since translated into more than 30 languages. It was launched in Scotland by Nicola Sturgeon. The manifesto aims to protect free expression for women by combating and eliminating the silencing of women worldwide.

"The worldwide effect of the PEN International Women's Manifesto was translated and distributed reaching 12.7 million which was a massive success and brought PEN into the world of writers.

"PEN international is a body of writers, they are our family and we collectively have a voice. Although small in number we continue to have enormous influence."

Irish PEN are working very closely with PEN International across a range of initiatives, focusing on the Freedom to Write campaign and others as the year progresses.

Launch of Women's Manifesto

Anne Enright, Senator Ivan Bacik and the Freedom to Write Campaign launched the PEN International Women's Manifesto in Ireland Sunday 18th November 2018 at Smock Alley Theatre.

With readings from Kerrie O'Brien, Kate Ennals and Liz McManus, four women writers were highlighted: murdered Mexican investigative journalist Miroslava Breach Velducea; murdered Mexican poet Susana Chavez; imprisoned Turkish-Kurdish painter and journalist, Zehra Doğan; and Palestinian poet, Dareen Tatour, recently released from an Israeli prison.

Irish PEN Chair Vanessa Fox O'Loughlin introduced the Manifesto and its principles. And Frank Geary spoke about the Freedom to Write campaign.

Day of the Imprisoned Writer

International Pen have designated the 15th of November as the Day of the Imprisoned Writer. Freedom to Write decided to highlight the plight of Ukrainian writer and filmmaker, Oleg Sentsov.

Oleg is serving a 20-year prison sentence on spurious terrorism charges after a grossly unfair trial by a Russian military court, marred by allegations of torture. He is currently being held in the 'Polar Bear' penal colony of Labytnangi, in Siberia, thousands of kilometres away from his home and family in Crimea.

The Freedom to Write campaign and Irish Pen believe that Oleg Sentsov was imprisoned solely because of his opposition to Russia's occupation and illegal 'annexation' of Crimea. We call on the Russian authorities to release him immediately and to respect Oleg Sentsov's human rights including the prohibition of torture and other ill-treatment, and his right to medical attention.

We called on the Russian Authorities to free all who are held solely for the peaceful exercise of their right to freedom of expression.

Blasphemy referendum

A letter from Irish PEN regarding the blasphemy referendum was sent to the press and circulated to members. Irish PEN supported the removal of the reference to blasphemy from the constitution.

The executive committee of Irish PEN, the Irish Centre for PEN International, has been campaigning for the offence of blasphemy to be removed from the Constitution since 2009.

It is essential to maintaining freedom of expression, ensuring that writers are free to criticise, that the offence of blasphemy be removed from the Constitution.

At a meeting of the writers in prison committee of PEN International in Brussels in March 2011, PEN Centres unanimously endorsed support for repeal of Ireland's Defamation Act.

INTO 2019

Join the committee!

We need a webmaster/social media maestro, an events planner, secretary, PR/press secretary and fund raiser!

All these roles need team players. If you have experience in any of these areas and feel passionately about rights for writers worldwide, get in touch! Email vanessa@writing.ie

2019 Irish PEN Membership

As a member of the Irish PEN, you support nearly 100 years of protecting and celebrating the freedom of speech across the world. Without your vital contribution, PEN would be unable to reach the incredible achievements it has today. Please help sustain Irish PEN by paying your fees! 2019 membership fee is now due and runs Jan to Dec, Full Members: €40; Associate members (unpublished or readers): €30. Students €10 (free access to all events)

To reduce costs and streamline membership we'd appreciate you subscribing via Paypal at www.irishpen.com (Become a Member section). To pay by standing order our details are:

Account Name: Irish PEN

Bank Address: Bank of Ireland, Smithfield, Dublin 7

BIC: BOIIE2D

IBAN: IE76 BOFI 9000 92240139 30

If you wish to mail in your payment, please send cheques for Irish PEN to:

Pádraig Hanratty
Bellurgan Point
Jenkinstown
Dundalk, Co Louth
A91 C9T3

Afterword

THE HISTORY and collection of inside stories on Irish PEN by J. Anthony Gaughan are a valuable addition to PEN'S global story. The very heart of the PEN mission believes in the transformative power of the written word and, there can be no doubt, Irish literature has changed the world. In Mexico, my country, Mexican writers were always fascinated by the relationship between Octavio Paz and Samuel Beckett and the anthology they did on Mexican poetry. W.B. Yeats is experienced as a writer close to Mexican sensibility through his idea of *Spiritus Mundi*. The interest continues in Mexico today as we read with passion the works of Colm Tóibín, John Banville, Emma Donaghue, Anne Enright and Paul Muldoon, among others.

PEN was one of the world's first non-governmental organisations and among the first international bodies advocating for human rights. We were the first worldwide association of writers, and the first organisation to point out that freedom of expression and literature are inseparable – a principle we continue to champion today and which is expressed in our Charter, a signature document, which manifests our ideals.

PEN also acknowledges the extraordinary bravery of those who write and speak truth to power in spite of great danger. The work which of course, is no problem, of PEN International and Irish PEN is more important than ever as thousands of writers are censured, live in peril, are forced into exile, and have been jailed unjustly and even been killed. It's interesting to note that PEN was founded in 1921 in the middle of James Joyce's struggle with censorship. Today he would be a writer in our Case List. Today his words continue to transform us.

JENNIFER CLEMENT
President, PEN International